Pigeon
with a
Bright View

Tallulah Banks

WESTBOW
PRESS®
A DIVISION OF THOMAS NELSON
& ZONDERVAN

WestBow Press books may be ordered through booksellers or by contacting:

WestBow Press
A Division of Thomas Nelson & Zondervan
1663 Liberty Drive
Bloomington, IN 47403
www.westbowpress.com
1 (866) 928-1240

ISBN: 978-1-5127-4994-6 (sc)
ISBN: 978-1-5127-4995-3 (e)

Library of Congress Control Number: 2016911650

Print information available on the last page.

WestBow Press rev. date: 03/20/2018

FOR MY GIFTS:
Adam & Rachell

MAY YOU BELIEVE TRUTH
THEN WALK IN IT

NOTICE

Due to the harsh living environment, there are a few references in the journal portion of this book, which suggests strong language. They are quotes from inmates and their implied meanings are intentionally included to preserve the accuracy of living in a correctional facility.

Contents

There are no numbered pages, let time "serve" you!

Introduction and Forward

I feel like my life over the past four years has been a series of quantum leaps. Each one unique, each one carrying me further still on my long nomadic journey. That journey included seven different stays at the Orange County Florida jail. It is through these experiences I learned that God can do so much in us when we are broken. It smarts to be corrected. Growth is messy and painful, but the Lord loves us so much. Sometimes we need a good spanking. He wants so much for us to reflect his character, that he will whittle the muck and sludge right out of us if we LET him. He wants to show us things we cannot see in our comfort zones. You will go through fire, but you will burn with care while the flesh is dying. The duration and severity of your flesh dying will depend heavily on how prideful, stubborn and hard-hearted you are. Sometimes, God will take us to the worst place, so he can lift us up to the best place. It took several grand swoops of whittling due to my over ruling strong will and rebelliousness. I lost my home, my children, my possessions and served 142 days of jail time on a Violation of Injunction/misdemeanor to fully grasp the following … .

Our life is not about us. It is about others and we must love them knowing they can be lost. Our life was not designed to have, get and acquire. We were created to love and worship our Creator. We were created to advance His kingdom. We do that by loving ANYONE in front of us. Join me in this journey.

7/24/00 Whitcomb Correctional Facility entry from 4th incarceration

18 women to a room. 2 toilets, 1 shower. It is always freezing, breakfast at 4a.m. Shampoo a luxury, food inedible. Most of the inmates eat very fast, probably so they don't taste it. I usually trade my food for paper and pens. I live in a pod like cell and there are 12 of these dorms. There is no such thing as black, white, rich or poor. We have all been stripped of everything we hold dear … pictures of our children, our jewelry, even our bras. They take our bras if they have any wire in them so we don't strangle anyone. Virtually all the floorboards in our pod are rotting. Filth is everywhere. There are giant black streaks on the ceiling to remind us of the quality of air coming from the vents. The windows only radiate light; they seem to be purposefully glazed over. You cannot see outside, only the bright haze of freedom gleaming to the inside dinge. We are sore for having to lie on our bunks so much. We are not allowed out of our cells much. Each mealtime becomes an anticipated event that breaks the monotony. When we get to go outside we are like excited schoolgirls. The sun feels so refreshing as it warms you from the inside out. I go to the shade where the pavement is not too hot. I lay flat on my back with my arms widespread in defeated surrender toward heaven. The blue sky swirls with fluffy white. The barbed wire frames the sky. I feel the wind blow and I know the angels are with me. My life feels normal for three seconds then I glance at my orange armband and blue coveralls. Reality coldly reminds me of where I am. Some of the inmates will put on skits to pass the time, usually a re-enacted drug deal with humor. They smoke from their tampons and laugh. Others play cards or sleep for escape, but there is no escape from the hand of God. I am grateful for that.

Definitions to help you along ...

C.O. ... Corrections officer

Chow. ... Meal Time

Prazzys. ... Prostitutes

Rec. ... 45 Minutes per day to go outside (subject to cancellation without notice or reason).

Pen ... Slang term for "jail"

Commissary: Order luxury items through the jail, such as Socks, underwear, candy ... Providing Someone on the outside can put money into Your account.

Violation of Injunction: Restraining order where you can't Go within 500 feet nor have Contact of any kind. (To do so Will result in your arrest).

Community Control: Similar to house arrest minus the Ankle gadget.

V.O.P: Violation of Probation. High chance you will go back to jail.

Section 1

Journal Entries

These entries are from my 7th and final stay in the Orange County Jail. I was arrested for a violation of injunction…the time where I grew the most.

This is the first day I have seen the outside world. This is the first day I have had paper. It is unbearable to not know how long I will be here. My bunkmate is a homeless woman who is only in her forties, but her hard life reveals someone twenty years older. Her name is Katrina. Her name is a familiar sound that offers warmth to me because I have a good friend with that name. The phones are broken—all of them. I won't be able to talk to any loved ones for Christmas. I can barely fathom what is upon me. I have requested transfer to the Christian facility. Father, be my advocate. I am determined to not lose my joy and to remember that these are just earthly circumstances. No one can crush me no matter how great the injustice. My Bible was confiscated upon booking. I yipped that this was a violation of my religious freedom, but her cold, inexpressive voice bellowed that the jail would provide one. I have yet to see it.

Thought for the Day:

Always remember your flesh is corrupt.

Memory Verse:

God's solid foundation stands firm, sealed with this inscription: "The Lord knows those who are His."

—2 Timothy 2:19

Yesterday was the first time the sun came out since I've been here. I borrowed a Bible to complete reading the book of Job. I'm still waiting to receive my Bible. I have requested a transfer to the Christian dorm. I sort of feel like I'm in *Dances with Wolves*. He's journaling about his strange, unwelcoming environment, narrating all along in the third person. I am lying in my bunk just looking around the cell at my bunkmates. I am gently reminded that I am with loved ones for Christmas. They are my sisters in Christ. Tonight ... Christmas Eve at the Whitcomb Correctional Facility, and in here I lie. I am alone amid my pity in my inner world. Two thousand Christmases ago there was no Andy Williams playing in the background, no burning fireplace with pretty stockings, no turkey thawing from Publix, and no Air Wick scents of apple cinnamon—just a baby! A baby born in filth, named Jesus. So here I am at Christmas—no Andy Williams, no hung stockings, no turkey getting ready to roast, and no pleasant scents of the holiday season. *Just Jesus.*

Thought for the Day:

> Long before you were ever conceived, you had an assignment on your life!

Memory Verse:

> The world and its desires pass away, but the man who does the will of the God lives forever.

> —1 John 2:17

My suffering is mounting. My heart is getting unbearably heavy. I requested to be moved to the chaplain dorm. They moved me to D dorm. This is for people trying to get their GED—duh! This dorm looks like an airplane hangar: thirty-two bunks in one large open room. I miss stuff I always take for granted—brown sugar oatmeal, taking a bath, a bowl of ice cream. I am desperately trying to find things positive this Christmas day. Let's see … it's not as cold in this dorm, and my bunk is the farthest from the day room area, so there is less noise. I was able to speak to my precious angels. They think I am on a missionary trip telling others about Jesus. My spirit is crushed beyond anything imaginable. I am still waiting on that Bible. Now that I have been moved here, I know no one. It is a savage jungle in here. Father, I am begging, pleading with you to please get me back home. Can I spend New Year's at home? Christmas lunch … green beans, fake mashed potatoes, something resembling roast beef, bread, and yellow cake with no frosting … well … ho ho ho to me!

Thought for the Day:

> Right now God is positioning you to bring you to the next "place." Be still so God has the space to move in you.

Memory Verse:

> "Before I formed you in the womb I knew you, before you were born I set you apart," says the Lord.
>
> —Jeremiah 1:5

We were issued sweatshirts today. A girl bonded out so I snatched her pillow and locker lock (I had neither). I got in trouble for whispering in line while going out to rec. An inmate named Donna gave me a pair of her socks. Thank God. We are not issued any socks, just nasty orange flip-flops. They keep it freezing in here. Someone told me it's to kill airborne germs. Another person insists it is to keep the inmates hovering in one place to minimize fighting. Last night one of the nicer COs brought in *The Grinch*—what a treat, two hours of feeling normal. After chow, sixteen of us were allowed to go outside (an area of about a thousand square feet with a twenty-five-foot barbed-wire fence), but since there are sixty-four of us, only those who can dart the fastest go outside. I ended my day with a lesbian inappropriately touching me when she walked by to get in line. It was gross.

Thought for the Day:

> Your flesh *has* to die. This is a requirement for spiritual living and growth. Remember, every believer has a ministry.

Memory Verse:

> The Lord is good, a refuge in times of trouble. He cares for those who trust in Him.

> —Nahum 1:7

The phones are back up—*yippee*. This afternoon a bunch of us got into trouble for standing in line to use the bathroom. The CO told us we were to be on our bunks by 1:55 pm., so she nitpicked us all to do extra chores because it was 1:58 pm. Oh bother, give me a break. I was assigned the bathroom with Darlene. After we were done we had to sit on our bunks for two hours in silence. Whatever. I'll just have me a pig fest with my bunkie. I'm gonna hunker down with my army blanket and have me some junk food I got from the Commissary. I'll slow my roll, but right now it's the only Christmas treats I got.

Thought for the Day:

> If you only focus on your situation, you will *always* be defeated!

Memory Verse:

> But because of his great love for us, God, who is rich in mercy, made us alive with Christ even when we were dead in transgressions—it is by grace you have been saved.
>
> —Ephesians 2:4–6

As the days pass I am more resigned to not fight this. It is feeling less and less like jail. Perhaps it is because I am mentally conditioning myself that I am stuck here due to a hurricane evacuation or that I am at a strict boarding school for the elite lower-middle class. I have made a few friends. Sharon is a middle-aged Caucasian crack addict on the outside world. In here though she is a friendly face I can chitchat with. This morning I had to see the nurse. They do routine TB and syphilis screenings. Ugh! I want to go home to my cat and uncomfortable beanbag bed. This is my seventh time here regarding an injunction. Each time my stay is longer as if building to some climactic end. Today marks the longest time. I know I won't wake up tomorrow and hear, "Bunk 10—pack it up!"

I can only wait for this bad dream to end. I am forever changed and will never be the same. What other time in my life will I ever be so connected with prostitutes, dope dealers, addicts, and thieves? A lot of women in here say they are saved. It is so easy for people to need God in here—we are broken and whittled down beyond what most will ever experience. I am confident I will start the New Year at the Orange County Correction system. It doesn't matter how unjust it is that I am here, I will not fight it. The wind has blown me here. I have food to eat, clothes to wear, and a place to lay my head. I want for nothing. God is providing my needs, and he is in control. My suffering will not go unnoticed.

Thought for the Day:

> When the Lord is going to use you for his glory, he must break you first!

Memory Verse:

> Let the beloved of the Lord rest secure in Him, for He shields him all day long, and the one the Lord loves, rests between His shoulders.

> —Deuteronomy 33:12

Today I was able to talk to Kit. She said my arraignment was January 2. It made me cry. Taking a shower was weird today. There were about twelve of us. It dawned on me, as I stood there naked, that several women (who were naked as well) are professing to be lesbians. Michelle was put into isolation for the night for making sexual contact with another woman. I wasn't afraid or uncomfortable really. I just went about my business. I don't have my contact lenses in, so there is a blur to everything anyway. Tonight I read all of 1 Peter. Lord, I know you are in control; I certainly am not. Tonight we had what is called a shakedown. We all get shuffled like cattle into holding cells while they tear apart our bunks with a vengeance. They are looking for what they call contraband. Saved food from chow, or washed clothes hung improperly. I hid my cross that Jesse made for me on Christmas Eve; it was made from grass blades. I was relieved to find it still intact. We were also strip-searched on this shakedown. I didn't stare intently, but you can't help it when you have sixty naked people in a fifteen-by-twelve room. It made me appreciate my body. The prazzys were by far the worst—completely worn out and haggard, and I'm not talking about their teeth. Although most of those were missing too.

Thought for the Day:

> God *will* restore what the enemy has taken, and when
> you get it back don't take it for granted this time!

Memory Verse:

> offer your bodies as a living sacrifice, holy and pleasing
> to God—this is your true and proper worship.

> —Romans 12:1

Another holiday approaching. Special days come and go while you are here. They are barely acknowledged, never celebrated. I am so starved for visual stimulation that I am actually watching a Lions' game. It reminds me of Thanksgiving with my boyfriend Randy and his family. I'm pretending I am there right now. It's a bit challenging though since I have no hot chocolate to drink and I can't hear the giddy chatter of Sabrina and Annette in the next room. I found out my pre-trial date is Feb 20th. Dear God, that's two months away. I am literally paralyzed all over. I can't move. I can't blink. I can't even cry. I just want to jump inside a snowflake and go to sleep.

Thought for the Day:

> The degree of Faith we have in God is the degree that we are at peace! Develop a hatred for sin.

Memory Verse:

> 2 Samuel 22:3
>
> My God is my rock, in whom I take refuge, my shield and the horn of my salvation. He is my stronghold, my refuge and my savior.

Today has been a horrendous day emotionally. I was denied bond. I very well could be here until February 20ᵗʰ. It is absolutely overwhelming, the very thought of having to stay here 60 days brings me to tears. This afternoon at Rec as I walked our square of freedom I cried uncontrollably. I kept crying out to God to rescue me, to throw down some justice. I had to sit down. I just buried my face trying to hide myself with my hair. In moments I felt hands touch my shoulders, another rubbing my back. 3 girls I had never talked to from another dorm offered their friendship. They were bi-sexual prostitutes but never the less I was really blessed that they bothered. I finally was able to pull myself together enough to finish my walk. Tonight a C.O brought in 2 movies and must have been having a great day because she said we could bring our blankets. I sat by this beautiful black girl who had just been transferred in. She had stitches on her forehead and was arrested for aggravated assault. She was rowdy but not in a threatening way. She turned to me and told me my hair reminded her of someone she knew. I kept looking at her intently too. She looked hauntingly familiar but I dismissed it with a "how in the world could I possibly know her?" She told me her name was Jenny. ... Then it clicked ... she had been my bunkmate on my 3ʳᵈ trip to Whitcomb cell 12. Once in cell 12 I sang to her and she was moved to tears as I grabbed her hand. I said some Oscar clip talk. The only thing I remember that I said was "Jenny our blood is the same color". I know this sounds trite but it was a really intense moment when you can bond with someone so hardened. I also had the girls believing I was an attorney in jail under cover to expose this and that. How ironic that during my marriage I was more a prisoner then, than I am right now at this moment.

Thought for the Day:

> Read the Bible like it was written just for YOU, because it is!

Memory Verse:

Hebrews 13:6

The Lord is my helper: I will not be afraid. What can mere mortals do to me?

Today I have been studying Romans. This dorm is like living on the streets. There is hostility everywhere and will unleash on you for no reason. I keep to myself a lot. I am learning in Romans 5:3-5 more of why I am here …

"We gladly suffer, because we know that suffering helps us endure and endurance builds character". Today I wrote my kids Ad and Rach. I was sad to write them. Sometimes the loss of my precious ones creep up on me like a quiet shadow. Then it runs over me and crushes me like a freight train. I will always hold to the hope of their restoration. The more I am here the more I feel like I am trapped in a building, wearing the same clothes day in and day out and being bossed around by a really mean babysitter. I am trying to let time serve me, not me serving time. Everything is in God's hands, not one detail escapes him. This afternoon Tabitha came and sat down next to me to talk (she gave me a handful skittles on Christmas day). She saw me reading the Bible so she just started talking about how she had given her life to Christ and all her struggles as a Christian. She has a 1-year-old son and the father is a big drug dealer. She expressed her desire to live right and make changes. She asked me about a church she had heard of so I gave her directions. Hopefully she'll go. On occasion I have observed her interacting with the other inmates … God is the farthest thing from their minds. Their perspectives are warped and the coldness from their hearts just oozes out toward everybody. I don't mean this in a judging way. It is these moments I realize I really have made some spiritual leaps. A process no doubt that will never be over until I get home (not home but HOME). Well I found another book to pass the time, Barbara Bush's autobiography. Her courtship with "Georgie" reminds me of Randy and myself. That 1940's sweet as pie thing. It gives me comfort to read it and takes me to brighter days. Tonight I tried to call the kids. Their father hung up on me three times. How can a man purposefully separate a mother from her children? It hurts so badly. I was feeling depleted when Jamie (an inmate I shared a pod with on the 3rd time here) started talking to me. Well her conversations are more like f--- with a few nouns thrown in for good measure. I couldn't help pull out of my low mood when she abruptly asked … "Are you gay?" "No" I told her with a half smirk. She quipped she was and had been all her life. She bumped shoulders with me and told me "don't be gay, they will break your heart worse than a guy!" Alrighty then … I am so homesick, so homesick I want to cry.

Thought for the Day:

> Share your testimony. … People can experience growth through your spiritual breakthroughs.

Memory Verse:

> Habakkuk 3:19

> The sovereign Lord is my strength; He makes my feet like the feet of a deer, He enables me to tread on the heights.

Tonight I will see my beloved through a glass wall, not the greatest set up but I'll take it. This morning someone is doing a puzzle by my bed. There is a big emblem of Star Wars on the front. It was like Randy was right here with me. My bunkmate Cristie went to court today, they offered her probation on a breaking and entering charge. I know this sounds strange but I don't want her to go. She is such an emotional rock, cheerful and friendly. A combination you don't find in here. I need to write a poem today. … Remember let time serve me. Well I got my first 5ᵗʰ grade gang up. Gigi walked by my bunk limping and I asked her if she was ok. There were three inmates in the same bunk area that taunted out she was "faking". I looked at Gigi and said that people are so hateful here. OOOH look out. I felt like I was getting flogged on the playground in 1982. A couple of screw you's and I am such a child … ok then. They have been snotty to us ever since. People overact with such a vengeance. It reminds me of elementary mentalities. By the way Gigi was bit by a brown recluse thank you very much!

Thought for the Day:

> If you get offended or annoyed easily, then you are operating in the flesh … cuz ya can't wound something that is already dead.

Memory Verse:

> Psalms 19:8

> The precepts of the Lord are right, giving joy to the heart. The commands of the Lord are radiant, giving light to the eyes.

I am so restless and discouraged. It feels like I cannot make it one more day. My body aches from being so cold and confined to my bunk. As I write this I can barely contain my tears. I know I am not but I feel so alone. Everyone who loves me is so far away.

This day has been the ho-humiest day. There was no rec, don't know why. I haven't had a shower in three days. It seems so pointless. I don't "hang" out with the girls in the day room. … everyone is too uptight and explosive. On rare occasion I'll play Uno with Gina or put a puzzle together. I wish I could get in my car and drive to the store because I want ice cream or even take a hot bath … WOW Queenie just tossed a snack at me. Cheese bits and popcorn … what a treat! Nights can be comforting; as an inmate will lead us in what is affectionally called "Lift ups". We each take a brief turn giving praise reports, sing a quick song or give a prayer request. Afterwards Lisa will lead us in the Lord's Prayer. Personally I think it's a feeble attempt to rebel against the C.O to talk longer. At any rate it's a nice thought.

Thought for the Day:

> God extends His grace to us when we don't know any better. God extends His mercy when we do!

Memory Verse:

> 1 Corinthians 15:58

> Stand firm and let nothing move you! Always give yourself fully to the work of the Lord, because your labor in the Lord is not in vain.

Right now I am numb and empty. I am tired, weak, and broken. I am whittled beyond the bone; I am crushed beyond anything I have ever known. Prepare me God for this nomadic journey I am on. Oh Father how much more? You know the outcome; you know how many more days I must call this place my home. I am sorry you have not been my First Love. Draw me back to you more than I have ever experienced and closer than I have ever known. Search me and know me. Take Randy. Take my children. They are yours not mine. There are dozens of women here just like me. It doesn't matter what the crime, if they deserve to be here or not. We all want to go home, we all want to be with our children. I do not stand alone in this pain. It is difficult but I know I need to rejoice daily. God knows exactly what I need and he will correct and discipline me because I am his child and he loves me so much.

Thought for the Day:

> Satan hates you with a passion! Remember his main objectives are to kill, steal and destroy!

Memory Verse:

> John 13:35

> Jesus said, "By this all men will know you are my disciples, if you Love one another."

This morning I was transferred to the Christian Dorm. My new bunkmate is Jill. She is from London. She was on her way back home from the States when airport security found some cocaine in her suitcase. Oopsey, she was sentenced to 2 $^{1/2}$ years for trafficking. Since I am now enrolled in a dorm that offers Bible completion classes by mail, I earn 5 days off my sentence a month for good behavior and 6 days off for being in the program. I am here for a V.O.P (violation of misdemeanor probation), which means I am not sentenced to do time. Nevertheless at this point nothing will hurt. I have been assigned to bunk #59 and on the top of course. This bed is only like 2 feet wide and a good 6 feet off the ground. There is nothing but hard cement to land on. My other bunkmate to my right is Colleen. She is in here for a drug and prostitution charge. She is so beautiful, Disney and apple pie looks. She is also infected with HIV.

Tonight we had another service. It was unreal. Everyone was crying, some on their knees, others running up and down the corridor shouting alleluia. So many being set free.

Donna and Ms. Swanson sang us goodnight. It felt good to take the focus off myself. Tonight is the first night I went to bed happy.

Thought for the Day:

> Want God more than you want air. What are YOU willing to do to get to Him?

Memory Verse:

> Psalms 95:2

> Let us always come into His presence with thanksgiving

What a day. I just want to go to sleep. Today during class the C.O went around and checked everyone's bunk. I didn't know it but we are not allowed to have things under our mattress. I had all my folders with my poems and journal entries and pictures of the kids. She coldly threw all my stuff in the garbage. I got up in the middle of class (a big no-no) and went to her pleading, crying and begging. I could not believe what she was doing. She sent me to a holding cell for over two hours. Later after she patronized me, she gave my things back. The C.O has not let us shower today, another thing to control. Last week a C.O went around to all the bunk lockers, if our locks were unlocked she fastened them all to the pay phone wires. Of course mine was one of them. A gesture meant to humiliate us. Tonight we have more class. This Christian dorm is a lifesaver. I am so weary. This has been by far the hardest thing I have ever had to endure, I know though it's good to see the bottom sometimes. I hope my children will go to bed happy tonight. Today in the holding cell I wept and wept and wept. I forced myself to sing virtually the entire time. The Lord spoke quietly to me ... "I have sent my angels in this cell with you just rest at my feet" ... I am on the verge of tears at any given moment. Tonight a couple came to speak. They led us in praise and worship. Our stupid orange flip-flops and blue suits praising the Lord. Not even being in jail would rob us tonight. Hands were lifted high and tears flowed. We still held onto our joy even at the bottom.

Thought for the Day:

God sees the heart ... man just sees!

Memory Verse:

1st Kings 2:3

Observe what the Lord God requires: Walk in His ways and keep His decrees and commands ... so that you may prosper in all that you do.

I feel sick! I think I ate too much crap. I give the rest of my commissary away; I couldn't look at it any more. I want to know what it feels like to keep my feet warm again. Every night I go to bed with freezing feet and my stomach growling of hunger pains. Granted that's due to being served supper at 4:30 in the afternoon. Outside today I witness my first and hopefully last lesbian encounter. Katrina kissed her girlfriend at rec. It was quietly cuz they would get in so much trouble! Nothing fazes me anymore. I continued to lean my head back and just let the crisp blue sky envelop me.

For a moment I am able to block the fence and barbed wire out, even the inmate's voices weave into the wind and fade.

Tonight has been emotionally tedious. I keep telling myself I've got to write another poem. I wallowed for a good 40 minutes before I said to myself … you're strong, sit up and just do it. I forced my non-committal pen to record my thoughts. I cried with each word jotted.

Thought for the Day:

>   Be a healer! Not a wounder!

Memory Verse:

>   Psalm 27:14

Wait for the Lord; be strong and take heart and wait for the Lord.

Last night the choir sang before service. Stephanie wrote all the songs. There are 9 of us and I am the only white girl. Today I am finding it so hard to keep my joy. I am so weary! It is in these moments the Lord reminds me how necessary this suffering is so he can complete a work in me. Daily I remind myself that these are only earthly things and I am just passing through. I want your presence to fill me. I want to feel joy here in jail! It is easy when I am surrounded with all my comforts and freedoms to feel joy. Lord saturate these tears with your joy and strength. I know I am free even in a jail. This stupid jail is just walls, a rundown building

Thought for the Day:

> Whatever struggle you are going through now will NOT break you! God will manifest His glory through your circumstance.

Memory Verse:

1 Peter 3:13-15

> Even if you should suffer for what is right, you are blessed. In your heart set apart Christ as Lord. Always be prepared to give an answer to everyone who asks you to give the reason for the hope that you have.

I have now spent 28 days in jail as a prisoner, a captive, an inmate bound by bars, possessing nothing! YET …

I have had freedom this entire time:

Free to praise God's name
Free to saturate myself in His Word
Free to worship
Free to sing His praises
Free to Love Him
Free to serve Him
Free to know Him
FREE. Praise God I am Free … … on the Inside!

Thought for the Day:

> If you have something that is separating you from God.. … Lose those shoes!

Memory Verse:

> Psalm 71:20-21
>
> You will restore my life again, O Lord; from the depths of the earth. You will again bring me up and increase my honor and comfort me once again.

I have not written my thoughts in a few days. I think it is because I am just so drained at the end of the day. My flesh is dying so fast I am exhausted. A process that will not stop until my flesh has turned to DUST! A shell left of a woman I no longer recognized. PRAISE GOD for that. I don't know what I will be or how I will be used, but I know it will be glorious! Yesterday in chow line, the woman ahead of me looked back at me. She just looked at me so tenderly for a minute or two. Without saying a word, she put her hand on my cheek and smiled. It was such a soothing gesture. Here I am at the close of one more day. One more day of being whittled, one more day of life on this planet and one day closer to going home.

Thought for the Day:

> Any time God shows you something new about your life … You have made progress! Remember every trial you overcome increases your understanding

Memory Verse:

> Isaiah 41:17

> The poor and needy search for water but there is none. Their tongues are parched with thirst, but I the Lord God will answer them; I, the Lord God of Israel will not forsake them!

We never have any toilet paper in this dorm! I'm sure it is because we use it as Kleenex as we are always crying. We are not always crying because of "where" we are, but because what God is doing in our lives. Praise and worship times are always so profound. That is when He breaks down walls, hearts and minds. We didn't have any classes today though. We had another shakedown. Well at least this time we weren't shuffled into a small holding cell naked. A couple of the girls were sentenced today. Deb has to do 5 years (home in 3) and Shelby got 35 months. I rest that I won't ever be doing that kind of time. I can't imagine, I just can't imagine. My heart is so heavy … Deb has 2 kids.

Thought for the Day:

> God does not force anyone to obey Him. He does and will allow things to get desperate for us. Remember LOVE brought you to jail!

Memory Verse:

> Colossians 3:2

> Set your mind on things above, not on things of this earth.

This will be a feeble attempt at a journal entry. Today marks day 34. This journey is getting harder and I feel like I can press on no more. I am withdrawn and cry uncontrollably. I know that God is breaking me down so he can use me. He is at work chiseling off all the muck and sludge in my heart. God has everything under control and I know He is holding me in the palm of His hand. My dying flesh though feels: alone and forsaken. I find comfort when I am in God's Word but only for that moment that I am reading it. I'm struggling beyond anything I can contain. There are inmates here who have been here 9, 10, 11 months, some going on to prison to do much longer time. Why am I still fighting this? I must be content no matter where I am and for the time being I am an inmate in the Orange County Jail. I am spiritually being feed, and I am safe … yet I can barely keep from drowning.

Thought for the Day:

The three doors we let strife come into our lives:

-   The Mouth … What we say to ourselves and others
-   Our Pride … We think we know it all and close our hearts to receiving valuable guidance and feedback.
-   Dissension … arguing often with others.

Memory Verse:

Psalms 84:11

For the Lord God is a sun and shield. No good thing does He withhold for those whose walk is blameless!

I am one day closer to freedom. One day closer to being home. I just need to rest, there's nothing more I can do. I spoke to Tabitha some more. She shared openly with me. She just got out of jail three months ago. The prostitution and drug charge violates her community control probation. She is certain it will be revoked and will be faced with back-to-back sentences. She knows how it works. She has been coming to jail on and off since she was 15. More on than off, sad to say. This afternoon in service the girls spurred me on to sing. I sang, "God bless the child" by Shania Twain and "We've been waiting for you" By Carolyn Arrends. Tonight our butch C.O. made those who didn't lock their locks run 5 laps around the dorm. Naturally I participated.

Thought for the Day:

There is no high like the most High!

Memory Verse:

1 Peter 5:7

Cast all your anxieties on the Lord; because He cares for you.

The Dorm choir has grown to 15 people. I told Grace I didn't want to participate any more. I kind of feel bad, I can't put my finger on it but my heart is just not in it. It's a luxury to go outside. I don't want to spend the only 45 minutes out of a 24-hour period I get practicing the same song twenty times. They are going to have a secret ballot to nominate two leaders to oversee the choir. Jill went around the dorm and took peoples nominations. Mimi told me some of the girls wanted to nominate me. I just laughed and asked "why?" "Because you are so humble," she chirped. A character trait in me that is evident to others? Wow! Thanks jail. 23 more days.. … 23 more days.

Thought for the day:

> When we are living as a true child of God, He is obligated to keep His promises. When we chose to not live right, God is not obligated! It is then only out of His grace to keep His promise.

Memory Verse:

> Ezra 8:22

> The gracious hand of our God is on everyone who looks to him.

In the early hours of the night 6 inmates were taken to D.O.C (prison). The prison bus comes with no warning! I heard any person that gets a sentence over one year transfers out from county jail and goes to prison. It was like a kidnapping! No one saw or heard nothin! It sucks because I didn't say goodbye! Crap! Suzanne and Deb are such on fire believers. I will miss sitting behind Sue inspiring me on to worship! Her heartfelt cheerleading moves to the Lord really blessed me! Today they are no longer a prostitute and cocaine addict. They are forgiven and written in the Lambs' Book of Life. It is so hard to have them leave. They both have encouraged me so much, both so strong to do their "time". I only see joy exude from them. Later tonight Linda a very mean spirited and grumpy inmate, tattled on me for standing on the toilet to look in the mirror. I was put in a holding cell for several hours. There was another inmate in the holding cell but she was asleep. All I could do was cry and pray through my brokenness. The Lord reminded me how much Christ suffered and he did nothing. What He was forced to endure and what glory He has now. I continue to give God the glory and all the praise through my tears. I am thankful I truly am, I just want this to be over. I love you Jesus, you are my life.

Thought for the Day:

> Pride will ultimately destroy your capacity to Love. It will eventually move you to exclude instead of include, and to judge rather than to serve.

Memory Verse:

> Proverbs 13:10

> Where there is strife, there is pride, but wisdom is found in those who take advice.

Our commissary didn't arrive today. They said it was because of inventory. Poop, I am really jonesing for a Reeses cup! Tomorrow is February 1st. Thank God, now each morning I can say to myself … "I'm going home THIS month". I am half way through this. My trial date is 2/20. I have left several messages on my attorney's machine to get me a bond hearing before the trial. I can never get through! My mind is so flooded on the possible outcomes. I just need to concentrate on resting in the Lord. I know this already. I guess I get discouraged on not seeing any manifestation of my prayers. I have surrendered everything to Him so he may move as He sees fit. Whatever gives God the most Glory is what I wish, no matter what that looks like. Sure would like some chocolate about now!

Thought for the Day:

> Sometimes we've got to go "through" it in order to get "to" it!

> Remember God does not dwell in a hardened, unclean heart.

Memory Verse:

> Isaiah 54:10

> "Though the mountains be shaken and the hills be removed, yet my unfailing Love for you will not be shaken. Nor will my covenant of peace be removed." Says the Lord who has compassion on you!

Today is Saturday. There will be visitation in a couple of hours. It is very difficult to get someone in. You are only allowed to pick 4 people and all the inmates are scrambling to pick specific days. I managed to sign up Kathy and Randy. They came to see me today. It's so hard to hear because you are in this little room with other inmates. You have to talk through little holes in the glass. You are not allowed to get out of your seat or the visit will be over. I was so happy and overwhelmed to see them. I'm glad Wanda fixed my hair for the visit. Now there is a worn out jail pastime. … Every corner is a make shift beauty parlor. I even cut a girls hair. Later I went outside for Rec. It is amazing how exciting it is to see an airplane fly by, hear birds chirping and watch rolling gray clouds. Kami (habitual petty theft offender) drew for me a picture of Jesus. I have it taped up to the ceiling of my bunk. It falls down a lot because I'm using the sticky packaging part of my whopper wrapper. I have made a deal with an inmate named Jonnie. She has no money in her commissary so I will get her some hair gel and she will give me her orange shorts and t-shirt. She is going to be transferring to prison soon and they won't let her take that. She shared with me some of her past. Let's just say this is my first friend who is a convicted murderer. She was sentenced to 2 years because it was ruled a justifiable homicide. (A relative was molesting her son). She is here now for violating her parole on a different charge. I don't remember what. My entries are getting less frequent. Perhaps because my time is drawing to a close. Well I am running as fast as I can toward Jesus, with or without Randy.

Thought for the Day:

> You learn forgiveness, by being hurt over and over again. Press in to the pain and walk through it. God can work in us the most when we are broken.

Memory Verse:

> Ephesians 5:2

> and walk in the way of love, just as Christ loved us and gave himself up for us as a fragrant offering and sacrifice to God.

Today marks a new beginning. Last night Randy ended our eight month courtship. We were both crying. It was awful. I do not understand. Randy said, he had felt pressed for days to break up. He kept arguing with God to not do it, but Randy has incredible discernment and always walks in obedience. He told me that God was trying to show and teach me things but that Randy was standing in the way of that. He told me how much he loved me but encouraged me that I need to put all my trust and all my faith in God and God alone. I did go outside tonight to get some fresh air. I did my usual laying on my back and prayed. I asked the Lord to continue to reveal himself to me. A minute later I turned my head to look up at the sky. There was not one cloud in the sky except for the four clouds that had aligned perfectly to form the features of a man's face. There was a "cross" like pattern in one of the eyes. I soaked it in and then closed my eyes with a heavy breath. Tears rolled down my cheek. After a few moments I looked back to where the face appeared, it was gone! The only thing that remained was a small patch of distorted cloud off in the distance. I felt a warmth wash all over me and I knew I had just been in the presence of the Lord.

Thought for the Day:

Give … … Give … … Give …

Memory Verse:

Psalms 119:2

Blessed are those who keep God's statutes and seek Him with all their heart.

I spoke to Dad today. His voice sounded so strange, raspy and high pitched. I pressed him until he told me. "The Doctors think I might have cancer, I didn't want to tell you while you are in jail." I immediately started crying. Dad said he was going on Friday for specialized tests. I asked Dad if he had ever accepted Jesus into his heart. Long pause. … "No Tallulah not really". I did not want to push the issue. He was a devout Catholic who went to mass every Sunday. Maybe they should call it "Mask" instead of mass. He went to church for 40 years, How is this possible? How is it that no one ever introduced him to Jesus Christ in all that time? I took a gentle approach and asked him to please ask Jesus to come into his heart. He assured me with a sincere "I will work on that ok?"

It's hard to believe that in a few days this Whitcomb journey will come to an end. I am a different woman than the woman who was arrested and booked December 20th 2001. I now know that to surrender all the way, not just the easy stuff is why I was pruned with such loving precision. Total surrender encompasses areas you do not want to let go of - things you don't want to turn over and take a chance of losing. I tell you it will cost you everything! But you will gain everything too! When I leave this facility, I don't want people to see Tallulah. I want them to see Jesus. After all, that is what we are called to be … Christ with flesh on.

Thought for the Day:

> Never set a timetable on anything! When we do that we
> rob God the space to move in our lives.

Memory Verse:

> Exodus 14:14

> The Lord will fight for you; you need only to be still!

The supervising warden paid a visit to our dorm this morning. He shouts out "anyone here with the last name Banks"? I piped up! I said I was Banks,Tallulah. The warden told me someone named Stan needs to speak with me. The chaplain took me in her office and we placed a call to my brother Stan. God bless him, he tracked me down. "Dad is dying" he said. With that, I fell into the chair. He went on to tell me Dad had a large tumor in his liver. It was twice its normal size and his spleen was starting to shut down. Dad got on the phone, I am crying hysterically and he could barely utter an audible tone … and these were the last moments I ever had with my Dad:

Me (crying): Daddy Hi. I love you and I am so glad that you were on this Earth!

Dad: I love you

Me: I will see you in my dreams tonight ok?

Dad: I always see you in my dreams.

Me: Dad ask Jesus into your heart! Promise me.

Dad: I promise. I am holding my rosary right now.

Me: I love you, Dad!

Dad: I love you too! I'm sorry things ended this way. Tell Adam and Rachell good-bye and I love them. I'm signing off now … I

Thought for the Day:

Love anything knowing it can be lost!

Memory Verse:

James 4:14

What is your life? You are a mist that appears for a little while and then vanishes!

Dad is barely hanging in there. The Doctor thought he would have passed in his sleep with the amount of morphine he is getting to numb the pain. I am getting ready for court. It's about 6:30 am. Gigi is going also. I know I will be released tonight. I took a plea so I could go see Dad. I plead No-Contest to hostile contact. I get time served and one-year probation. I have had 60 days of humbling and whittling. I can give up the right of being right for my father's sake. Gigi and I were transported handcuffed in a van with no windows, just baby peep holes. The security is very tight. We were also fitted with a steel chain around our waist, then it looped around and attached to our handcuffs. It gave us minimal movement. We asked the C.O why such extreme measures? She responded with flat effect "So you or any other inmate can't put us in a choke hold and try to kill us!" I won't take that one personally. We were moved to another holding cell with 4 or 5 other women to wait our court time. One hour passes, and then another one. Gigi and I kept ourselves pretty entertained. We made up songs and sang worship tunes. The acoustics were incredible, nothing like solid concrete to meet all your concert needs. The judge had fallen behind so we were not taken into the courtroom until 9:45 a.m. After the slowest 15 minutes of my life my name is called. My Public Defender went through the plea bla bla blahs. She petitioned the court to let me leave the state as my Dad lay dying. Motion granted. Dad died at 10:07 a.m.

Thought for the day:

> When someone comes against you it is NOT the person,
> it is the enemy.

Memory Verse:

> 1 John 2:5

> But if anyone obeys his word, love for God is truly made complete in them.

Section 2

The Seven Day
Spiritual Journey

I have heard it said more than once that a "pigeon" is a filthy, dirty bird, and it carries many different diseases. Then you have us ... the human ... dirty and full of disease as well, which we infect to those around us ... for us, it comes in the form of hardened hearts, bitterness, resentment, our tongue and bla bla bla bla bla. I could use this entire page rattling off adjectives which describes our traits and how these traits shatter and destroy. We are such desperate sad people. We look in every nook and cranny to fill up our brokenness don't we? We search and we search ... trying and doing anything we can get our hands on. For you, the precious reader it may be crack or hooking, booze, pills, hate, revenge, money, status, control. ... For me it was pot! I was out of control; wherever I was I couldn't wait to be home so I could light up a joint ... and ooohhh the release, the escape, and no more pain ... I could cope with the loss of my children. I could feel normal, relaxed, and peaceful. Then in 2 to 6 hours depending on the quality and how fat the joint was ... there I was again ... broken, no let me say that again ... BROKEN!

You may also be feeling that same overwhelming sense of loss. It does not matter the source or root of the pain, brokenness is brokenness! The first step in your seven-day spiritual journey is to invite the one who was murdered for you to enter your heart! Murdered so you no longer have to remain a pigeon, stuck in the filth of your sins. Don't you know you are a child of God? God loves you so much, so much that he bled on a cross with nails wedged through his hands and feet. Right now I want to ask you to go to a quiet place and just read these words aloud.

"Jesus, I come to you with an unclean heart, with a mind full of anger and hate. Please search me and know me ... Right now I turn my whole life over to you. ... The alcohol, the drugs, my crimes ... I don't want this life Father. Please enter my heart and cleanse me of who I used to be. Fill me up with your presence, with your joy, peace, and your love. I ask you to put only people in my life who are good for me and good to me. I love you Jesus, reveal yourself to me as I begin my relationship with you. Amen!" Ok, that was step one. Now, are you ready for some hard-core spiritual growth? This next step may sting! You might feel the toes stepped on a bit here.. ... Stand with clay feet for the next seven days and walk through the hurts. Peeling off the tattered and useless layers is no fun. However it is necessary and critical to your spiritual survival! Remember Satan is not going to give you up without a fight! He is a liar and a thief. He has no ownership over you! You do not belong to the enemy and he can't have you! Stay strong and you will have victory, you are a Child of Light!

Day 1:

When a baby is born, there is this essence of perfection ... you know what I mean? We come into this world with no emotional damage or negativity. Then we grow up and are at the mercy of those who raise us. What I'm trying to say is we're all screwed up here! We beat ourselves up over and over again ... I'm a disgusting fat pig ... I'm so stupid. ... I'm the ugliest person on the planet ... whoa! Stop it right now! The first day of our spiritual journey we are going to spend this time re-programming our minds.

Get a piece of paper and write down every awful thing you have ever been told about yourself. Include your own negative personal beliefs.

Once you are finished read them off to yourself. Take ALL those hurts, resentments, and disappointments and funnel that energy to your hand. Now scribble a HUGE "X" over the whole page! You know why? It's all a bunch of crap that's why. You are a beautiful, precious child of God! No negative thing comes from God, so I dare say a spirit of anger, a spirit of bitterness, a spirit of malice etc. COMES FROM THE ENEMY!

Spend the next few minutes meditating on a Love letter that someone wrote to you:

> *"You may not realize it, but I know everything about you. I know when you rise up and when you sit down. I am familiar with all your ways for you were made in my image. I chose you when I planned creation. You were NOT a mistake; for all your days are written in my book. It is my desire to lavish my love on you! I want to do this because you are my child and I am your Father. I offer more than your earthly father ever could. Every good gift that you receive comes from my hand. I am your provider and I meet all your needs! My plan for your future has always been filled with hope because I love you with an everlasting love. My thoughts for you are as countless as the sand on*

the seashore. I rejoice over you with singing. I will never
stop doing well to you for you are my treasured possession!"

Psalms 139:1-3, 15-16

Genesis 1:27

Acts 17:28

Ephesians 1:11-12

Zephaniah 3:17

1 John 3:1

Matthew 7:11, 5:48, 6:31-33

James 1:17

Jeremiah 29:11, 31:3

Exodus 19:5

Day 2:

Today we are still trying to get the internal sludgy layers to fall off. We can't do this in our own strength. Most of us are so tattered and train wrecked inside we can barely function through our day. It's so cool to know that God holds us in the palm of His hand! We usually don't recognize this because we are too caught up in "trying" to make things happen or manipulating a situation to go our way. The following scriptures are for you to meditate on as you embrace "WHO" you are in Christ!

Remember in 2nd grade when we had to write our spelling words out 10 times? It stunk, but there is something to be said about repetition! Get a piece of paper and pen and write the following verses 5 times each. As you write meditate on each one.

I am a child of God. (Romans 8:16)

I am forgiven. (Colossians 1:13)

I am a new creature in Christ. (I Corinthians 5:17)

I am delivered from the powers of darkness. (Colossians 1:13)

I am kept in safety wherever I go. (Psalms 91:11)

I am an imitator of Jesus. (Ephesians 5:1)

I am a laborer together with God. (I Corinthians 3:9)

I am healed by His stripes. (I Peter 2:24)

I am establishing God's word here on earth. (Matthew 16:19)

I am observing and doing the Lord's commandments. (Deut. 28:12)

I am an inheritor of eternal life. (1 John 5:11)

I am exercising my authority over the enemy! (Luke 10:19)

Day 3:

Understand that spiritual growth and maturity will continue through your whole life ... You will never "arrive". It is a process that will not cease until the moment you take your last breath. I have said many times throughout this book that our flesh needs to continually be put to death! Now this is not a one-time deal where you say a special prayer and you're covered until retirement! Every single day, holidays included you are to die to self! Look there is good in this world and evil in this world. Good = Jesus and Evil = Satan. The enemy can take on many forms. I'm not saying he turns himself into Jimmy Stewart or something. The enemy is too subtle, so much so that you won't even see it! When you feel hateful, jealous, greedy, depleted, depressed, fearful, confused, belligerent, rebellious, spiteful, sarcastic, selfish, arrogant, judgmental, restless ... These are all demonic influences! Satan uses you to achieve a means. He battles to control your mind. One of his ways to kill, destroy and steal from you is through inhabiting our minds! I have some incredible news for you. ... You have the authority to beat him. It is through the blood of Jesus Christ we bind back and rebuke his strongholds. Meditate on the following verses.

Psalms 91:13
You will tread on the lion and the cobra; you will trample the great lion and the serpent.

1 Thess 5:23
May God himself, the God of peace, sanctify you through and through. May your whole spirit, soul and body be kept blameless at the coming of our Lord Jesus Christ.

1 Corinthians 2:16
"Who has known the mind of the Lord so as to instruct him?" But we have the mind of Christ.

Day 4:

Ok we talked about character traits that come from the enemy. Let's chat about how we can reflect God's character. The Lord refers to these traits as "fruits" of the spirits. If you were to plant an apple tree in your yard and each season yielded you tons of beautiful sweet red apples wouldn't you say that tree bore many good fruits? (I know that was a run on sentence but I don't care). Ok what if that same tree rarely grew apples and the apples that did grow were sour tasting puny with worm holes in um awful! What a useless tree huh? See where I'm going with this? These are the fruits of the spirit:

LOVE
JOY
PEACE
PATIENCE
KINDNESS
GOODNESS
MERCY &
SELF-CONTROL

As a child of God we must strive to attain these. We don't have a choice; Jesus commands this! Take time to evaluate each character trait. Dig deep this could sting. On a piece of paper answer the following. … Which ones are hard for you? Why? Time to dig deep. A moral inventory is in order. Do you lack any? That answer requires a hard core moral inventory to find the roots and sources of the above characteristics you are void of.

Pick two character traits you want to improve on. Now make a plan on paper how you are going to do that! Remember that book the "Love Dare"? … yeah something like those plans of actions.

Day 5:

Today is going to be a little more meat and potatoes than previous days. We are digging deeper huh? Trying to find the gold in you that's being purified! I hope you are seeing things clearer now that you have some insight on spiritual warfare. It is critical that you have a protective covering placed over you. This daily prayer covering immobilizes the enemy and he is forced to retreat. You should speak it aloud! Use your authority over the enemy with vigor!

Heavenly Father:

I pray this prayer in the power of the Holy Spirit and in the name of Jesus Christ. I bind all curses that have been spoken against me. I bind and render useless all prayers not inspired by the Holy Spirit. I take authority over Satan and all his demons, and those people who are influenced by them. I declare Satan is under my feet and shall remain there all day. Satan you are bound from my family, my mind and body. I claim a hedge of protection by the blood of Jesus, around myself, my spouse and my children (names) I ask you God to dispatch your angels to surround me. I ask all of this in Jesus name. Amen.

Good Stuff huh?

Day 6:

How would you define the definition of "delivered"? I think of words like … Set free, rescued … yea that about sums it up. You have just recently been enlightened and Satan's scam for your mind has been exposed. Whether you know it or not you have layers of strongholds over you. We need to pray a prayer of deliverance. Through Jesus you can also break generational curses (sins that pass down from your parents and their parents … like addiction, alcoholism, pornography etc. Buckle your seat belt!

Lord I come to you as my deliverer. I repent of all my sins and the sins of my ancestor that have caused curses to come down on my family line. I refuse to accept anything from Satan and loose myself from every dark spirit and command them to leave now in Jesus name. In the name of Jesus Christ, I now break and loose myself and my children from any sickness or disease. I loose myself from every ungodly soul tie that is hindering my growth. Lord I now ask to be filled with the Holy Spirit That I may have the power to fight against the devil and overcome temptation. I also ask to be filled with your love, wisdom and understanding. I ask this all in Jesus name! Thank you Lord for making me free on the inside!

Day 7:

Whew! I don't know about you but I feel lighter. Now what? Well there is of course the obvious ... ... Stay in the word daily, get plugged into a church, no more hanging out with the old crowd, no more jail, make it a point to only surround yourself with good Godly people. Even if that means you move to Ohio to get away from your old way of living ... Then DO IT! There is something though much greater than these! Your ministry! You have purpose, you have a destiny, and you have an assignment on your life. Spend time in prayer and ask the Lord to put an anointing on your life and that you will be willing to do all that God has called you to do. You will slowly feel these little stirrings in your spirit. These stirrings are being placed there by the Holy Spirit. Pray for God to ordain encounters and open doors of opportunity for you. You sure have a powerful testimony ... how can you use your experiences to give God glory and advance His kingdom?

Now go relax and take a nap or something.

Section 3

Inmate Portraits and Poems from Jail.

A Box of Cornflakes
Trapped in a Cranberry
T. Banks

I sit within
My nicely decorated palace
Trapped in a fancy cell
Paid no mind to my gut
Screaming to run
I murdered a child who had no voice
To save a cowardly imp
The moon beckons me to freedom
Though tempted I hither not
I sleep within walls
That hold only pain
I serve my sentence
For two little lights
My youth fades with each tick
My soul shuts down
Seasons come and go
Little lights still need me
But I can swim no more
Unbridled freedom comes
If am willing to drown

King Henry
T. Banks

Thy blood is black
So black as night
You plot like a viper
To crush her in flight

Your hatred just simmers
Festers and stews
Your light a mere glimmer
That thrives on his takes

Evil lurks in your soul
Weeds grow through your heart
Your arrogant sins
Will set you apart

You are but a fool
Who enjoys doing wrong
My angry king
Will sing you no song

You will go back to the earth
To ashes and dust
To rot in a hole
That is justice enough

Kamoloka by Theosophist:
A Homecoming for Dad
T. Banks

Calmness dances in my eyes
As the wind whispers comfort to me
The specter of death rises to my conscious state
My soul contains infinite wisdom
As the brightness and warmth encompass me

I grasp the whiteness
While I ponder this euphoric freedom
Gentle forces pull me into its luminance canopy
My essence is all that remains
Spiraling upward I soar into Delta State

The power of thought surrounds me
I sense harmonious nurturing
As beams of love and companionship join me in flight
The celestial light weaves together
In magnificent symmetry

Still shifting to and fro
A musical tingling radiates through me
I'm carried past the astral planes, into the heavens
Summoned further still as the circle of light expands
A guiding warmth reaches out to me
And there is peaceful understanding of why I am HERE

Mama, Ninah & Helper Bug
T Banks

Twirl me around mama
Can I fix your hair?
Dance in my dreams
Make me fly
Get on your feet
Catch this ball
Boy I am tall
I come all the way up to ... here
Swing me high
Touch the sky
Ride that train
Why does it rain?
Little bear
Ladybug doll
Get me my tiger ...
Please
Cut my hair
Do I dare
To ride this ride alone?
Pet the horse
You know of course
How much that I love you
Glad I was there
For your first rainbow
I did wipe some tears
Soon a missing tooth
Then another one loose
Here comes Christmas Day
Long to hear you say ...
But I won't
Until the day
You fly back my way

I'll leave the light on
My precious angels

Baby Mine
Tallulah Banks

The thunder roars with anger
The fury of rain pounds at the ground
The wind howls in pain
As the animals search for her
The trees shake in sadness
Can you hear the tears?
Blowing against the roses?

Tis two magnificent trees
A kaleidoscope of leaves
Your names embossed on each
The tingling of the light
Is felt by mother earth
Nature reveals its emptiness
As a mother searches for her little ones.
Peace will not come until she holds them.

Water
T Banks

I am a mere bird
Without a nest
A bear
Robbed of her cubs
I am a city without walls
Fragile as a spider web

Oh to escape …

And climb inside a snowflake
To be a petal on a flower
Or a color in the rainbow
So the fangs of the wicked
Might cease

I can only rest in the dust
And wait for the
Bishop of my soul
To refresh me like cool water
In the summer

Empty River
Tallulah Banks

The rain spills downward from the
Heavens
For a thousand tears are falling
The angels weep for a mother
Without her little ones

The sky, a blanket of somber gray
As with her heart without them
She relishes for the moment
She can embrace her tender ones
Forever

Time is all she has contained within
She feels nothing but the hollow
Emptiness
Of her soul
Precious ones so far away
Only in dreams can she touch them
The only place there's dancing
The only place she smiles

Broken Leaves
T Banks

For what is my purpose?
I have nothing
I want nothing
Only you my precious angels
My existence futile without you
I carry you with me
But tis not enough

I long to stroke your tender curls
To rub your flawless face
Dance again in the rain
Swing you under a rainbow
What simple pleasures I took for granted

Tis etched so deep within me
Let me not fade from your heart
I am with you, I am here
Please touch me in your dreams

A Broken Heart

4:00 A.M
Tallulah Banks

Faint hues of the moon
Shines down my silver path
The coolness of the wind
Filtrates through me
Blood of an innocent man
Washes over me
Amidst my depleted vigor
Withered as fading grass awaiting fall

I was a stone
But the water of my tears
Has grinded me to sand
Oh sustainer of the universe
Maker of heaven and earth
I am whittled to the bone

Worms feed sweetly at my flesh
Like a grave preparing to receive me
Keeper of eternal flame
I feel your presence in the thunder
As waves of pain pierce in sweet surrender

You did not make me
Only to destroy me
My almighty one I plea
Let the pillars of heaven tremble
With your whisper of justice

1969
T Banks

Comfort me
Hold me
Love me
I'm wounded
I'm bleeding
Take my suffering
I lay it down
The cold is calling
I won't answer
My heart knows the truth
Pain setting in
I release it to you
Move me to the mountain
I'll hide till the morning
Keep my heart in a jar
Is what I wish to do
Safe from the offender
But I belong to you
Feeling you holding me
Love wrapping around me
I rest in my unshakable king

Red Headed Bear
T Banks

The wind blew me to you
A mere bird with no nest
Small hands reached to me
Kindness engulfed me
It was you
That poured into me
When I was too whittled
To care
It was you
A clay Stone
Who brought back my smile
Amidst a mothers loss
Precious Baby Bear Friend
You may think you are weak or
Some compass off course
But even the rain knows not
Where it falls
Yet covers the earth
And makes things grow tall
You were my raindrop
And I needed you so
For without you …
This tree could not grow

What is HorseDust?

HorseDust is the essence we leave behind to everyone who crosses our path. Jesus told us that we are to be bright lights. That we are to shine from the inside out to whoever is in front of us. HorseDust are the seeds we plant, the impressions we make, and hopefully the love we have shown. It is through all this that lives are touched and changed forever. So UNLEASH YOUR LIGHT

Last thought:

> A TREE GIVES GLORY TO GOD BY BEING A TREE ... ARE YOU GIVING GLORY TO GOD BY BEING YOU?

About the Author

Tallulah has a Bachelor's in Psychology and a Master's in Public Administration. She is also the founder of Horsedust Productions – a ministry dedicated to uplifting people in fun and innovative ways. This book contains an intimate and up-close look at life as a prisoner

Printed in the United States
By Bookmasters